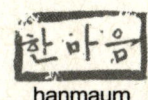

A Thousand Hands of Compassion

The Chant of Korean Spirituality
and Enlightenment

Korean Translation by Seon Master Daehaeng
English Translation by Hanmaum International Culture Institute

Illustrations by Hyo Rim
Book design by Su Yeon Park
Published by Hanmaum Publications
Tel: 031-470-3175 / Fax: 031-471-6928
onemind@hanmaum.org
www.hanmaum.org/eng

First Edition October 2008
Third printing December 2008
Second Edition June 2009

© 2009 Hanmaum Seonwon Foundation
All rights reserved, including the right to
reproduce this work in any form.

Printed in the Republic of Korea

ISBN 978-89-91857-13-1(03810)

```
국립중앙도서관 출판시도서목록(CIP)

만 가지 꽃이 피고 만 가지 열매 익어 = (A) thousand hands
of compassion : 대행큰스님의 뜻으로 푼 천수경 / 한글번역:
대행 ; 영어번역: 한마음국제문화원 ; 그림: 임효. — 2판. —
안양 : 한마음출판사, 2009
    p. ;   cm

ISBN 978-89-91857-13-1 03810 : ₩20000

천수경[千手經]

223.59-KDC4
294.38-DDC21                         CIP2009001577
```

만가지 꽃이 피고 만가지 열매 익어
대행큰스님의 뜻으로 푼 천수경

한글번역   대행큰스님
영어번역   한마음국제문화원
그 림   임효화백
디자인편집 박수연

출판등록   384-2000-000010
전화   031-470-3175
팩스   031-471-6928
홈페이지   www.hanmaum.org
E-MAIL   onemind@hanmaum.org

발행   한마음출판사
발행일   2008년 10월 한·영문 초판
           2008년 12월 한·영문 초판 3쇄
           2009년 6월 한·영문 2판

ⓒ2009 (재)한마음선원
본 출판물은 저작권법에 의하여 보호를 받는
저작물이므로 무단 전재와 무단 복제를
할 수 없습니다.

ISBN 978-89-91857-13-1(03810)

Introduction

A Thousand Hands of Compassion has been popular in Korea for the last 1,300 years. Compiled from different sutras, it integrates all of the major elements of Korean Buddhist thought into a single text that is chanted daily in temples throughout the country.

Seon Master Daehaeng takes the traditional elements of this sutra — mantras and Pure Land faith, repentance and the vows of a Bodhisattva — and shows us a path of awakening. For in its essence, *A Thousand Hands of Compassion* is a description of the enlightened life and the determination to follow such a life. It is life seen through the eyes of an enlightened one. It is life open to the unlimited compassion and ability within us. It is the life of one who smiles and refuses to submit to the control of fear and desire.

As we chant or recite this text, we are affirming that we also are such beings, and we are affirming our connection to all other beings. For although we may seem separate and disconnected, each cut off from the other, all beings inherently share the same life. All beings inherently share the same wisdom and enlightenment as all Buddhas. All beings are inherently connected through our fundamental Buddha-nature. Hearing and feeling this truth, if all beings began to put this into practice, we may one day wake up and discover that our world has transformed into the Buddha's Pure Land!

About this text

This English translation is based upon Seon Master Daehaeng's contemporary Korean edition of *The Thousand Hands Sutra*(千手經). For centuries, *The Thousand Hands Sutra* was written in a combination of Sino-Korean characters*(hanmun)* and phonetic renderings of the Sanskrit mantras. Thus it was very difficult for ordinary people to approach the meaning of the text. Seeing this, Seon Master Daehaeng said:

This sutra encompasses all of the fundamental principles and truths of the universe. Yet if someone just recites the text with no awareness of the underlying meaning, how can it resonate with them, how can it help them, let alone the greater world around us?

들어가는 글

대행큰스님의 뜻으로 푼 천수경(千手經)이 임효 화백의 그림과 만나 『만가지 꽃이 피고 만가지 열매 익어』라는 눈부시리만치 아름다운 시화집으로 새롭게 탄생하였습니다.

천수경은 천년이 넘는 세월 동안 한국인의 마음에서 마음으로 입에서 입으로 면면히 이어져 염송(念誦)되어져 왔으며 오늘 날까지 한국 전역의 사찰에서 매일같이 독송(讀誦)되고 있는 경입니다. 원래 천수경은 한문과 산스크리트어 진언의 한자음역으로만 되어 있어 일반대중들이 그 깊은 뜻을 헤아리기 어려웠습니다. 그러나 대행큰스님께서는 "온 우주가 돌아가는 참된 에너지가 담겨 있는 경(經)을 그 깊은 뜻도 모른 채 앵무새 마냥 읊조리기만 한다며 이 세상은커녕 내 마음조차 울리기가 힘들다" 하시면서 30여년 전에 천수경을 쉬운 우리말로 풀어 놓으시어 누구나 독송을 하면서 그 뜻을 충분히 마음속에 새길 수 있도록 하셨습니다. 1년전, 대행큰스님의 뜻으로 푼 한글 천수경을 영문으로 번역하기로 결정한 후, 원문 천수경과 이미 외국학자들에 의해 영어로 번역되어진 천수경 영어본들을 대조해 보면서 저희는 큰스님의 명쾌하면서도 깊고 정확한 뜻풀이에 다시 한번 놀랄 수 밖에 없었습니다.

평소에 이해하기 어렵다고 여겨지는 경(經)을 시(詩)의 형태로 소개한다면 일상생활 속에 그 가르침이 자연스럽게 녹아들 수 있으리라 생각했기에, 대행큰스님의 한글뜻풀이와 영어 번역본을 그림과 함께 엮어 한편의 시집으로 제작하기로 하였습니다. 불자가 아닌 일반대중들이 이 책을 보더라도 그 가르침이 저절로 느껴질 수 있는 책이 되기를 고대하면서 말입니다. 그 과정에서 지난 30여년간 한국화 부문에서 한국인의 마음세계와 동양정신의 진수를 함축적으로 화폭에 담아내기에 심혈을 쏟아온 임효 화백의 작품과 조우하게 되었습니다. 처음부터 천수경의 내용과 너무나 완벽하게 어울리는 임효 화백의 작품을 바라보면서 과거생의 선연(善緣)이 맺어놓은 신묘한 결실이 아닐까 싶어 가슴속 깊이 감사할 수 밖에 없었습니다.

So some thirty years ago, relying upon her own profound experiences and insight as an awakened master, she sat in meditation and produced a Korean edition in modern language that speaks to modern people.

The translators would like to thank Seon Master Daehaeng, the many sunims of Hanmaum Seon Center, and all of the countless people who have helped with this book and shown their support in so many ways. For it was only through their support that this undertaking was possible. We would also like to thank the Venerable Gwang Wu Sunim and the poet Ko Un for their generosity and kind words.

What words can express our deep gratitude to the artist Hyo Rim for his rich and wonderful artwork? Infused with his bright spirit, it provides a poignant accompaniment to Master Daehaeng's text. As one looks upon his illustrations, the ideas of true self and non-duality don't feel so far away after all.

May all beings awaken to the infinite light
ever shining within them.
With palms together,
Hanmaum International Culture Institute
January, 2553 (2009 C.E.)

큰스님께서 풀어내신 천수경에 담겨 있는 무량무변의 에너지와 한치의 걸림 없는 마음으로 자신의 그림을 흔쾌히 보시해 주신 임효 선생의 지극한 마음이 하나로 어우러져 새로운 모습의 천수경 책이 나오게 된 것입니다. 이러한 마음의 힘이 담겨 있었기에 이 책은 오랜 전통의 유럽 출판계 전문가들의 마음에 강렬한 인상을 남기며 그들의 마음을 단숨에 열었습니다. 이 책을 펼쳐보는 모든 분들이 페이지를 한 장 한 장 넘기면서 천수경의 글과 그림을 볼 때마다 삶의 지혜와 영감을 무한히 얻어갈 수 있기를 간절히 발원하며 정성을 기울였던 저희들의 바램도 함께 이루어지는 순간이었습니다.

처음에는 불가능하리라 여겼던 모든 일들이 때로는 하늘이 내려준 것과 같은 바람을 타고, 때로는 온 힘을 다해 노를 저어 여기까지 올 수 있었던 것 같습니다. 이처럼, 저희들이 얻은 많은 것이 흐르는 물처럼 이 세상을 위해 원만하고 자연스럽게 회향될 수 있도록 소중한 도움을 주신 모든 인연들께 마음을 모아 깊이 감사 드립니다. 더불어 뜻으로 푼 천수경에 부쳐 귀하고도 수승(殊勝)한 글을 정성스럽게 써주신 광우스님과 고은시인께도 심심한 감사를 드립니다.

한마음국제문화원, 한마음출판사 일동 합장
불기 2553년 (서기2009년) 1월

About Seon Master Daehaeng

Seon Master Daehaeng was born in Seoul, in 1927, and is widely regarded as one of Korea's foremost seon(zen) masters. She awakened at a young age and spent the decades afterwards applying what she experienced.

For many years she had struggled with the question of why people suffer. Seon Master Daehaeng realized that ultimately the answer was ignorance. People were unaware of the non-dual foundation that connects all existence. Unaware of this inherent connection, people lived as if they were disconnected from everyone else. Unaware of the ever-changing nature of reality, people tried to grip and immobilize that which is ever flowing. Unaware that their foundation is endowed with all of the ability of the universe, people thought themselves weak and helpless, limited to the kindness of others or the ability of their intellect.

Thus, people suffered because their behaviors and thoughts were not in harmony with the underlying truth of our world. And because people didn't know about this inherent foundation, with its infinite ability, they also didn't know how to free themselves from the suffering they had made.

So Seon Master Daehaeng began teaching people to entrust and let go of everything that confronts them to their inherent foundation, and then to go forward while observing. By continuing to apply and experiment with what we understand, a small grain of faith can grow into a great ball of flame that burns up all attachments and habits of the body and mind. Once this cloud of habits and discriminations has lifted, our inherently bright, true nature can shine through.

While seon masters have traditionally taught only monks and a few nuns, Seon Master Daehaeng was determined to teach spiritual practice in such a way that anyone, regardless of their occupation, gender, or family status could practice and awaken.

With this in mind, in 1972 she established Hanmaum Seon Center as a place where everyone could come and learn about their true nature and how to live with freedom, dignity, and courage. And even today, she is still there, teaching only this.

대행큰스님에 대하여

한국 불교의 뛰어난 스승님들 중의 한 분이신 대행큰스님은 1927년 서울에서 태어나셨습니다. 스님은 일찍이 자성을 밝히시고, 증득하신 바를 완성하기 위해 10여년이 넘는 세월을 산중에서 보내셨습니다.

스님은 수년간 '어째서 사람들이 고통 속에 살아가는가?'라는 문제를 쥐고 씨름하셨습니다. 근본자리를 통해 본래부터 일체가 서로 연결되어 있음을 인식하지 못한 채, 사람들은 마치 따로따로 떨어져 있는 양 살고 있었습니다. 그 어느 것도 멈추는 순간 없이 부단히 변화하고 있는 현실의 본질을 인식하지 못한 채, 사람들은 쉼 없이 흘러가고 있는 것을 고정시켜 손에 쥘 수 있다고 여겼습니다. 누구나 내면에 무한한 능력이 있는 근본을 지니고 있다는 사실도 모른 채, 사람들은 스스로 유약하고 아무런 힘이 없으며, 타인을 배려할 여력도, 지혜도 없다고 생각하였습니다. 사람들은 세상이 돌아가는 진리와 조화를 이루지 못한 채 살고 있었고, 자신들이 본래 지니고 있는 근본에 대해서도 몰랐으며 고통으로부터 자신들을 벗어나게 할 수 있는 방법 또한 몰랐기에 어렵게 살 수 밖에 없었던 것입니다.

대행큰스님은 닥쳐 오는 모든 것을 근본 자리에 맡겨 놓고 관(觀)함으로써 스스로의 문제를 스스로 해결할 수 있는 법을 사람들에게 가르쳐야겠다고 단호히 결심하셨습니다. 이렇게 해서 스님은 1972년, 누구든지 와서 자신의 근본자리, 참 성품에 대해 배우고, 자유롭고 당당하며 씩씩하게 살아갈 수 있는 법을 배우는 도량으로 한마음선원을 세우셨습니다. 근본을 믿고 거기에 놓는 작업을 우리가 실생활에서 끊임없이 활용하고 실험하다 보면, 처음에는 작은 낟알 크기만했던 믿음이 점차 거대한 불덩어리로 커지면서 우리들의 모든 집착과 습(習)을 태워버리게 됩니다. 그렇게 되면 우리의 본래 성품이 뚜렷이 밝아지면서 찬란한 빛을 발하게 됩니다.

스님은 우리 모두가 자성을 밝혀 최상의 지혜와 능력을 얻으신 부처님들처럼 될 수 있는 잠재력을 가지고 있음을 누누이 강조하십니다. 대행큰스님은 오늘 날까지도 여전히 직업과 성별과 사회적인 지위에 상관 없이 법을 물어오는 모든 이들에게 깨달음을 얻을 수 있는 지혜를 나눠 주시며 한마음선원에 주석하고 계십니다.

Preface

People often try to find some special meaning in life, but there is no such thing. Life just is. It doesn't need some additional meaning. Unfortunately, unenlightened beings fill their lives with so many useless labels and speculations.

As they struggle under the burden of the masks they create and their endless judgments about themselves and others, the pain they suffer seems to reach down into our very planet. It is for them that Daehaeng Sunim has given this incomparably profound teaching.

Daehaeng Sunim penetrates this sutra to its essence, with nothing superfluous. Through her explanations even people whose eyes and ears are still dark will be able to taste the truth.

Her explanation of the Sanskrit core of *The Thousand Hands Sutra*, "The Great Dharani of Wondrous Phrases," overflows with the unconditional compassion and love of the Bodhisattva Avalokitesvara.

The Thousand Hands Sutra has been chanted in Korea for the last 1,300 years by uncountable spiritual seekers. Its structure is unique because it was compiled by taking outstanding verses from the sutras and patriarchs, and then adorning the core mantra front and back with these verses.

In her modern Korean translation of *The Thousand Hands Sutra*, Daehaeng Sunim has given us a true taste of Seon(Zen). Further, until now it has been chanted only in Korea, but through this translation Daehaeng Sunim has made these deep teachings available to people throughout the world. How truly wonderful!

As people chant this sutra, absorbing Daehaeng Sunim's teaching that any awareness, any awakening can only come through our fundamental mind, our inherent nature, I am sure that uncountable numbers of people will awaken to the truth.

Gwang Wu Sunim
Former President of The Bhikkuni Council
The Jogye Order of Korean Buddhism

대행큰스님 뜻풀이 천수경에 부쳐

중생은 의미 있는 삶을 추구하지만 삶에는 무슨 의미가 있는 것이 아닙니다. 삶은 그저 존재하는 것일 뿐, 그것은 어떤 의미를 지니고 있지 않습니다. 중생의 삶에는 얼마나 많은 의미가 따라붙고, 또 얼마나 불필요한 가정이 많습니까?

수많은 가면과 거추장스런 아상(我相)과 인상(人相)들이 맞붙어 뒹구는 이 고통 받는 행성에 사는 중생을 위해 대행스님은 깊고 가없는 가르침을 베풀어 오셨습니다.

대행스님이 풀어 놓은 경전들은 군더더기가 없고 진리의 핵을 단번에 꿰뚫어 놓으셨으니 눈 멀고 귀 먼 자라 하더라도 접하기만 하면 진리의 참 맛을 알 게 될 것입니다.

대행스님이 풀어 쓴 뜻풀이 천수경은 신묘장구대다라니(神妙章句大陀羅尼)라는 천수다라니가 그 핵심인데 관세음보살의 더 없는 자비와 사랑이 스며있습니다. 1,300년을 내려오며 많은 수행자들의 입에서 입으로 염송(念誦)되어 온 천수경은 편찬부터 독특한 구조를 가진 경전으로 불교 경전과 조사스님들의 가르침 중에 귀감이 되는 구절들만 가려 뽑아서 다라니의 앞과 뒤를 장엄하였습니다. 바로 그 점이 천수경의 특징입니다.

한국불교에서만 독송되고 있는 천수경을 대행스님이 선적(禪的)인 언어로 뜻풀이를 하셨고 거기다가 여러 나라의 언어로 번역해 책을 만들었으니 참으로 반가운 소식입니다. 그 어떤 깨달음도 다 근본 마음자리, 본래 성품자리에서 나오는 것이라는 대행스님의 가르침과 함께 천수경을 독송하여 부디 많은 사람들이 진리에 눈 뜨게 되길 기원해 봅니다.

대한불교조계종 前 전국비구니회 회장
광우(光雨)합장

Foreword

by **Ko Un**

Look at that! A thousand hands dancing!
Dancing hands of compassion.
Behold Master Daehaeng's dance of compassion,
going far and wide.
So radiant!

Who is a bodhisattva, what is a bodhisattva?
If a bodhisattva can't help the beings that are here
right now,
is such a person really a bodhisattva?
A thousand times No!
A true Bodhisattva
calls forth unconditional incomparable compassion
holds nothing back,
and saves the lives in front of her.
Behold,
like a thousand moons shining in a thousand streams
all flowing flowing,
Bodhisattvas shine forth pure light upon all.

And seeing so many still unable to free themselves
from a thousand kinds of suffering and pain,
how sad,
how sad,
the tender compassion of a thousand Bodhisattvas rushes forward.
Such far-reaching compassion,
the compassion of a thousand eyes,
not the two eyes tainted with desire,
but a thousand eyes overflowing with every aspect of compassion.
And not just two hands,
a thousand outstretched hands dancing far and wide.
And in the palm of each hand,
an utterly pure eye shining light on all before it.
So sincere,
so utterly sincere.
For over a thousand years in Korea
have people recited *The Thousand Hands Sutra*
with such perfect devotion and sincerity
as each new day dawns

추천사

고은

어허 일천의 손길 춤추는도다
자비의 손길 춤추는도다
보소서
여기 대행 자비무 너훌너훌 눈부시도다

보살이 그 누구이더뇨 그 무엇이더뇨
보살은 당장 제 앞의 뭇 생명이 아니면
천번도 더 보살 아니더이다.
그 뭇 생명으로 하여금
그 뭇 생명에의 가 없는 자비를
온 몸 바쳐 불러오는 보살이더이다
보소서
누리에 일천의 강물 흘러흘러
거기 일천의 달이 푸르게 비쳐 내리더이다
어디 그 뿐이리오
뭇 생명 일천의 괴로움 아픔들 오래 벗어나지 않노라면

슬피
슬피
일천 보살의 슬픈 자비가 거기 서슴없이 달려가더이다.
이 아득할손
일천의 자비여
오로지 두 눈의 욕업 아닌
일천의 눈 자비의 만상 넘치더이다
오로지 두 손 아니고
일천의 손길
일천의 손길 너훌너훌 춤추더이다
아니 그 일천의 손길 하나하나
그 손바닥마다 각각 청정지극의 눈이 빛나더이다
지극하더이다
지극하더이다

and as each day draws to a close.
And yet, for so long have people gone
without understanding this sutra's Sanskrit heart,
The Great Dharani of Wondrous Phrases.
"It's already a mantra, what need of explanations?"
But now is the time throughout the world
for every house and every person
to open doors and open minds
and for this sutra to be understood by all.
Now is the time for this ocean of life and all its waves to
join together
and carry this sutra's meaning far and wide.
Oh waves and troughs
and you empty spaces and spray above them:
Master Daehaeng is a Buddha of this world,
present in this world,
manifesting miracles throughout this world.
One with all beings, one with their suffering
and one with their ability to understand,
she illuminates the deep meaning
of *The Sutra of the Thousand Hands and Eyes of the Bodhisattva of Perfect Compassion*
revealing compassion like mother's milk
and love as tender as a mother's tears.
Now begins the feast of a thousand eyes
and a thousand hands!
This great virtue and grace,
first of all, it's easy
first of all, it's comfortable
first of all, it's warm,
this world that Daehaeng has opened for us.
In due course, the tide surges in,
and then goes out again,
carrying everything to all directions.
Now this tide has returned,
a thousand hands of compassion
dancing far and wide.

Ko Un

이 지극 귀명으로
무릇 일천 몇백년동안
동방의 그날그날 신새벽 먼동을 열고
그날그날 저녁을 닫으면서
애오라지 간절하디 간절한 가슴으로 읊어오더이다
새삼 이 천수대비주의 뜻
헤아릴 길 없이 읊어오더이다
과연 진언이건대
굳이 뜻을 낳을 까닭이 없다가
바야흐로 온 세상 저마다
집집마다 문 열고
마음 열어
뭇 생명의 바다 어우러지는 파도의 때이므로
이제 그 뜻 쉬이 널리 나아가더이다
이 파도와 파도 이랑들이여
이 파도 위 허공들이여 티끌들이여

여기 사바세계 영험의 보신
여기 사바세계 원력의 화신
대행노사의 회통으로
천수천안관세음보살광대원만대비심다라니경이
아기의 젖인듯
어미의 눈물이듯
일천의 눈
일천의 손 잔치 열리더이다
이 복덕과 더불어
첫째 쉽고
첫째 편하고
첫째 따뜻한 대행의 세상
때맞춰 밀물져 오더이다
썰물져 갔다가
밀물져 돌아오더이다 너훌너훌 춤이더이다.

고 은

A Thousand Hands of Compassion

The Chant of Korean Spirituality and Enlightenment

만가지 꽃이 피고
만가지 열매 익어

hanmaum

정구업진언 淨口業眞言

선업 악업, 좋다 나쁘다, 더럽다 깨끗하다 하는
망념들을 몰락 놓고 진실한 말을 하며 관觀하는 진언

진실한 말을 하면 진언이 되고

하치 않은 말을 하면

구업이 되도다.

A mantra
for realizing inherently bright nature,
speaking truthfully,
and completely letting go of delusions
such as good karma and bad karma,
like and dislike,
defiled and pure:

Speak from the truth

and each word becomes a mantra,

speak outside of the truth

and each word becomes karma.

오방내외안위제신진언
五方內外安慰諸神眞言

온 누리의 일체 부처님은 내 한마음에 계시오니
진실하게 관하는 이 마음이 바로 진언일세

온 법계에 두루 하온 내 한마음을

끊임없이 따르리다

진정코 믿으오리다.

**All Buddhas throughout all realms
exist at this very moment within my one mind,
sincerely relying upon my one mind
is itself a true mantra.**

My one mind

present throughout every realm,

ceaselessly I follow it,

earnestly I trust it.

개경게 開經偈

우리들이 살아가는 이 세상은 부처님의 세상과 둘이 아니어서, 항상 봄이 되어 꽃이 피니 향기의 문은 늘 열려 있도다.

일체 모든 부처님의 마음은

내 한마음에 깊고 깊어

한 찰나에 부처님의 마음이요,

한 찰나를 몰라서

끊임없는 억겁에 끄달리네.

The world we live in
is none other than the realm of Buddha.
Here it is forever Spring,
flowers bloom without end,
and the fragrant path is ever open.

The minds of all Buddhas are

fully present

within my one mind.

Buddhas' mind is realized in an instant.

Not knowing this instant

causes an eternity of suffering.

일체 모든 부처님의 마음이 내 마음이요

듣고 보고 행하는 그 모든 것

부처님 법 아님 없어

내 한마음이

바로 부처님의 법이며 생활일세.

The minds of all Buddhas are my mind.

Nothing I see, hear, or do

exists apart from

the truth they realized.

My one mind itself is the Buddha-dharma,

present throughout all aspects

of my life.

개법장진언 開法藏眞言

내 마음을 깨달아서 알고 본다면 사방이 터져서 그대로 여여하네.

들이고 내는 모든 것을

내 한마음에 맡겨 놓으니

거기에서 모든 것을

전부하네.

**If I truly awaken,
all directions burst open
and everything is utterly complete
just as it is.**

All things that arise,

all things that I do,

I entrust to my one mind

for it does everything.

**천수천안관자재보살광대원만
무애대비심대다라니계청**
千手天眼觀自在菩薩廣大圓滿
無碍大悲心大陀羅尼啓請

일체제불의 마음은 내 한마음이니,
내 한마음이 모든 법과 생활을 하도록 청하옵니다.

관음보살님

내 한마음에 계시오니

항상 감사하옵니다.

일체제불 원력이 내 한마음 원력되어

항상 일상생활 걸림 없이

해 나가게 해 주시니

감사하옵니다.

**The minds of all Buddhas are my one mind,
so I ask my one mind
to take care of everything in my life.**

Avalokitesvara,

the Bodhisattva of Compassion,

who hears the cries of all the world,

resides within my one mind.

How can I express my gratitude?

The great saving power of all Buddhas

becomes the saving power of my one mind.

With it I can live every day

free of entanglements.

So wonderful!

일체제불 자비한 손 내 한마음 손이어서,
내 한마음 손으로 유위법과 무위법을
둘 아니게 항상 움직이니
이 감사함을 어찌 말로 다하리까.

일체제불 밝으신 눈
내 한마음의 눈이어서,
한마음의 눈으로 전 우주를 두루 살펴
죽은 사람 봄으로써 산 사람을 바로 보니
두루두루 정확함이라.

The compassionate hands of all Buddhas
are the hands of my one mind.
Their touch harmonizes all seen
and unseen realms.
How can words express my gratitude?

The bright eyes of all Buddhas
are the eyes of my one mind.
Through their vision
see the entire universe as it truly is,
and by clearly seeing the dead,
fully understand the living.

일체제불 진실하신 마음이
내 한마음 진실하온 마음이니
무위 유위로
항상 길을 밝게 인도하시어
안 보이는 무위심 속에
일체 만법 귀중함을 베푸시네.

The deep sincerity of all Buddhas
is the sincerity of my one mind.
It always brightly leads me
using all manner of seen and unseen methods.
With infinite compassion it reveals
the precious truth of how everything
in the universe flows.

일체제불 마음이

내 한마음 법이오니

그 만족함 광대무변하도다.

삼심三心이

일심一心되니

몰락 전부 놓는다면

일심조차 세울 게 없도다.

The mind of all Buddhas functions

together with my one mind.

Endowed with everything,

encompassing everything,

it is utterly complete.

My past, present,

and future consciousness

all become one.

Completely let go of everything,

and even this "one" disappears.

천지의 근본도

내 한마음이 근본이요

태양의 근본도

내 한마음이 근본이라

어찌 모든 세상

두루 살피지를 못하리오.

온 우주의 근본도

내 한마음이 근본이니

둘이 아닌 세상을

똑바로 지도하도다.

The foundation of the Earth is my one mind,

the foundation of the sun is my one mind,

how could there be something

my one mind

isn't taking care of ?

The source of the entire universe is

my one mind.

It guides every single thing in this

interconnected world.

일체심이 곧 일심이니
찰나찰나 나투며 길을 밝히도다.

우주의 근본은
내 한마음이 근본이니
찰나찰나 나투면서
일체 모든 유생 무생의 길을
밝게 인도하도다.

All minds are one,
it manifests every moment
and shows me the path.

The foundation of the universe
is my one mind.
It manifests every instant,
illuminating the path for all beings,
both with life and without.

내 한마음

온갖 것의 근본 되니

근본에서 나온 것을

근본에다 몰락 놔서

밝은 마음 이루리다.

본래부터

마음에는 문이 없어

넘어들 것 없으므로

넘어갈 것 또한 없어

한마음이 근본이니

그대로가 생활이며 법이도다.

My one mind is the root of all things.

All things arise from it,

so all things I completely entrust to it.

This letting go

fills my heart with light.

Inherently there is no path to find,

nor obstacles to overcome.

One mind is the foundation,

so just as it is, it is truth

and fully present throughout my life.

일체제불 마음이 곧
내 한마음인 것인 줄 알았으니
내 한마음 지극하게 믿으오며
한마음의 진실한 뜻
따르오리다.

내 한마음 믿으오며
한마음의 진실한 뜻 따른다면
자유자재하리이다.

Knowing that the wisdom
and enlightenment of all Buddhas
is my one mind,
I fully trust my one mind
and follow its compassionate
guidance.

Believing in my one mind
and following its profound truth,
I will become free
from all attachments
and able to use
the infinite ability within me.

내 한마음 그대로 관세음이신 고로 내 한마음에 귀의하오니

이 한마음 믿고 믿어 원을 세우오니
일체가 다 이루어지이다.

My one mind is the Bodhisattva of Compassion,

so I return to my one mind and rely upon it.

Believe and believe in this one mind,

give rise to firm intention,

and everything will be accomplished.

내 한마음 그대로 관세음이신 고로
내 한마음에 귀의하오니

내 한마음 믿고 믿어 따른다면
지혜 물리 터져나와
자유법을 얻으리라.

My one mind is the Bodhisattva of Compassion,

so I return to my one mind

and rely upon it.

If I believe and believe,

and follow my one mind,

wisdom will burst forth

and the path to freedom

will become clear.

내 한마음 그대로

관세음이신 고로

내 한마음에

귀의하오니

오로지

내 한마음 믿고 따르면

찰나찰나 나투는

모든 중생 그대로

건지리다.

My one mind is the Bodhisattva of Compassion,

so I return to my one mind and rely upon it.

If I believe and follow

only my one mind,

I can become one

with continuously arising unenlightened beings,

and in so doing,

save them all.

내 한마음 그대로

관세음이신 고로

내 한마음에

귀의하오니

오로지

내 한마음에

모든 원을 세운다면

성불하리라.

My one mind is the Bodhisattva of Compassion,

so I return to my one mind

and rely upon it.

If I entrust all of the vows

I have made

to my one mind,

I will surely become

a Buddha.

내 한마음 그대로 관세음이신 고로

내 한마음에 귀의하오니

오로지 내 한마음에 모든 원을 세운다면

사방에 문이 없어 본래 내가 없기에

건널 것도 없는 것을 알 것이니

건널 것도 없다 하는

그 님을 찾으리라.

My one mind is the Bodhisattva of Compassion,

so I return to my one mind and rely upon it.

If I entrust everything I'm searching for

to my one mind,

I will realize that

the path I seek is in everything around me,

and inherently "I" does not exist,

so everything I'm searching for

is already right here.

I will find the one who says

that everything is already right here.

내 한마음 그대로 관세음이신 고로

내 한마음에 귀의하오니

산다 죽는다 하는 것은

고정된 참 모습이 아니기에

이승 저승 없는 한마음 되오리다.

My one mind is the Bodhisattva of Compassion,

so I return to my one mind and rely upon it.

"Living" "Dying"

Such things are not my true essence.

Thus I will become one mind,

which transcends all distinctions

such as realms of the living and the dead.

내 한마음 그대로 관세음이신 고로

내 한마음에 귀의하오니

마음의 공덕 계율 법행을

하루속히 이루오리다.

My one mind is the Bodhisattva of Compassion,

so I return to my one mind and rely upon it.

Virtue, precepts, and actions in harmony

with the Dharma

are all done through mind.

I vow to attain these without delay.

내 한마음 그대로

관세음이신 고로

내 한마음에

귀의하오니

본래 밝아

생과 사에 걸림 없는

길 없는 길 한마음이

하루속히

이루어지이다.

My one mind is the Bodhisattva of Compassion,

so I return to my one mind and rely upon it.

One mind,

the Way that isn't a fixed path,

its inherent brightness is never troubled

by birth and death.

I vow to realize one mind without delay.

내 한마음 그대로 관세음이신 고로

내 한마음에 귀의하오니

원하건대

일체제불이 도량의 집

내 한마음에 계시옴을 알게 하소서.

내 한마음 그대로 관세음이신 고로

내 한마음에 귀의하오니

마음은 고정됨이 하나 없이 평등하니

일체의 법성신이 내 한마음인 줄 알게 하소서.

My one mind is the Bodhisattva of Compassion,

so I return to my one mind and rely upon it.

Let me know that all Buddhas exist

within my one mind,

the place where enlightenment is attained.

My one mind hears and answers

all the cries of the world,

so I return to my one mind and rely upon it.

Mind freely manifests and functions everywhere.

Let me discover that all enlightened teachers

are my one mind.

내 마음의 칼산지옥도
한마음 능력 두루하여
스스로 무너지게 하소서.

내 마음에
화탕지옥 일으킬 때
한생각이 스스로 꺼지어
저절로 무너지네.

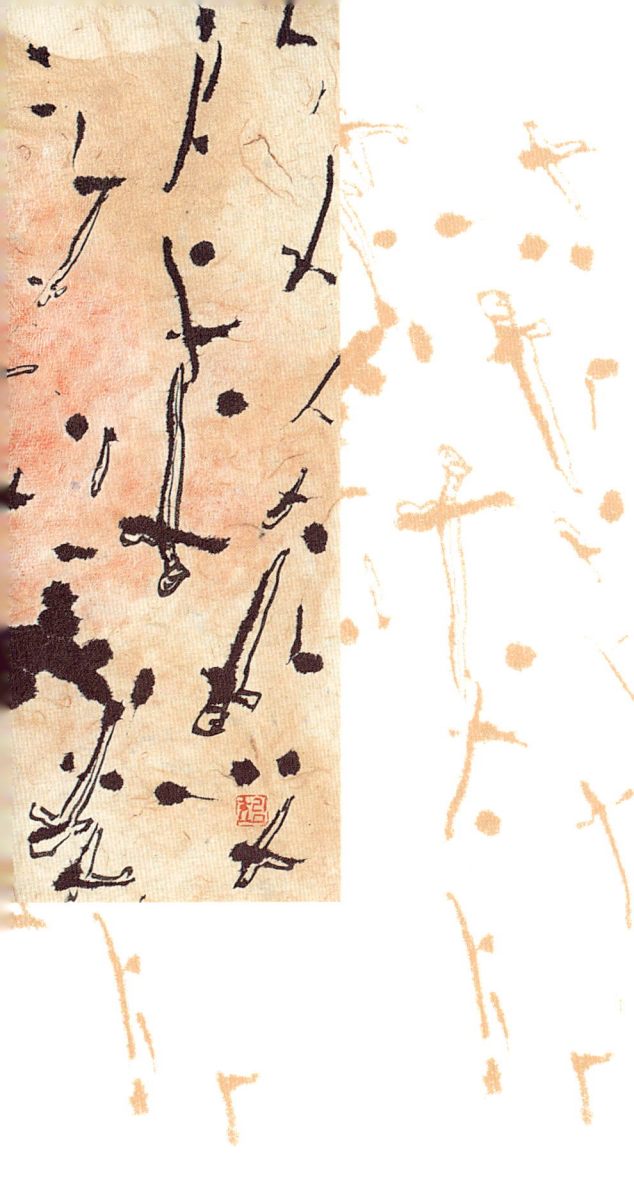

Should the hell of knives arise within my mind,

let the all embracing energy of one mind

cause this hell to collapse.

A single thought causes my mind

to fall into the hell of boiling water,

but when that thought is dissolved,

this hell also collapses.

내 마음의 지옥도 한생각이 스스로 꺼지어
저절로 무너지네.

내 마음이 귀신행을 한다면은
내 한마음이 귀신 항복 받아 충만하리.

만약에
아수라의 마음 일으킨다면
스스로 내 마음에 조복되리.

만약에
축생의 마음 일으킨다면
스스로 큰 지혜로 둘 아닌 도리를 알게 하소서.

All of the hell realms within my mind vanish

as the thoughts that gave rise to them

are extinguished.

When my mind acts like a hungry ghost,

my one mind can embrace that consciousness.

Experiencing oneness, it is truly fulfilled.

When I rely upon my one mind for everything,

should the mind of an evil spirit arise within me,

it will willingly surrender to my one mind.

Should the mind of an animal arise within me,

let me learn the truth of non-duality

through the deep wisdom of one mind.

유무세상 관하시어 보살피며 건지시는
부처님께 한마음으로 귀의하리다.

끝이 없는 대천세상 유생 무생 부처님과
한마음에 귀의하리다.

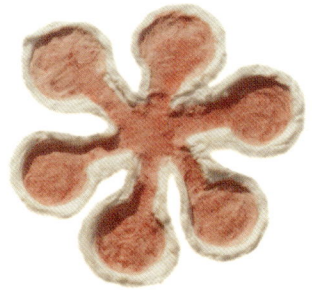

Through one mind I take refuge in Buddha,

who watches over and takes care of

all material and nonmaterial realms.

I take refuge in Buddha and one mind,

which encompass the endless universe

and all things with life and without.

끊임없이
천수로써 보살피는
한마음에 귀의하리다.

I take refuge in one mind,
with a thousand hands
it ceaselessly takes care of all things.

끊임없이 보살피며
여여하신 한마음에
귀의하리다.

I take refuge in one mind,
remaining just as it is,
it ceaselessly takes care of all things.

둥그런 큰 마음을
내시어서
두루두루 건지시는
한마음에 귀의하리다.

우주 세상 일체 생명
자재로이 보살피는
한마음에 귀의하리다.

I take refuge in one mind,
with all-embracing harmony
it saves all beings everywhere.

I take refuge in one mind,
which completely looks after all beings
throughout the world and universe.

시공 없는 한생각에
일체를 다 거두시는
한마음에 귀의하리다.

끊임없이
만물만생 항상 비춰 주시옵는
한마음에 귀의하리다.

I take refuge in one mind,
with a single thought
transcending time and space,
it nurtures all.

I take refuge in one mind,
endlessly giving light to all.

끊임없는 생명들의

줄어듦도 늘어남도

본래 없는

밝은 길을 인도하는

한마음에 귀의하리다.

끊임없이

전 국민을 보호하며

맛과 이익 주시옵는

한마음에 귀의하리다.

I take refuge in one mind,

it guides all life to the bright path,

which is neither longer nor shorter,

sooner nor later.

I take refuge in one mind,

always protecting us,

it enriches us

and gives us the taste of the Dharma.

없는 고로 큰 시방에
두루두루 한생각을 내시어서
보살행을 하심같이 한마음에 귀의하리다.

걸림 없이 일체 모든 크나크온 보배 자비
한마음에 귀의하리다.

유무 없는 중심 근본 스승하여
각覺 이루는 불성에
귀의하리다.

I take refuge in one mind,

free of all forms and shapes

it is able to become anything.

Like the love of a Bodhisattva,

the thoughts one mind gives rise to

embrace everything throughout all realms.

I take refuge in one mind,

the all embracing treasure of compassion.

I take refuge in Buddha-nature,

my center, foundation, and teacher,

which transcends existence and nonexistence,

and through which enlightenment is attained.

신묘장구대다라니
神妙章句大陀羅尼
자신의 묘법은 글귀 아닌 대원력이니

**The profound ability within me
is awakened not by words,
but by the determination to save all beings.**

이 소리는

나와 내가 같이 이 경지에 오고 감이 없이

부동지不動智의 큰 지혜를 굴리어

걸림 없이 굴리어 큰 바다와 같으니

진정 그 뜻을 알라.

고요한 물 흐름과 같이

제 마음을 한마음으로 이끌어 주옵소서.

오고 감이 근본에 있어

고요한 마음으로 이루오리다.

I and my true self,

together as one.

At this stage freely coming and going

without a trace,

able to apply great unshakeable wisdom,

using it without the least hindrance.

As vast as an ocean,

truly understand what this means.

Like quietly flowing water,

may my heart always flow

towards one mind.

Coming and going

are all done through the foundation.

With a quietly flowing mind,

I will become one

with my foundation.

우리들의 염念하는 소리

온 누리에 퍼지나니 살피소서.

부처님의 마음과 내 마음이

둘 아니게 인도하여

눈 아닌 눈의 지혜로 두루 이루어

살피고 살피소서.

The sounds of our reciting
spread throughout all realms.
Hearing this, may all Buddhas and
Bodhisattvas look after us.

Please guide me so that my mind
becomes one with the mind of all Buddhas.
With the wisdom of the eye that's not an eye,
please make this happen
and look after me.

눈이 없어

관觀하고 관하고

또 부지런하오리니

가고 가고

돌아 돌아

모든 고난이 큰 뜻으로

모든 액난이

몰락 사라지이다,

사라지이다.

Without eyes,

keep watching and watching,

diligently watching.

Going and going,

changing and changing,

meeting this great truth of emptiness

all suffering and disasters

fall away

and disappear

disappear.

모든 망상도

부동심不動心으로

스스로 스스로

마음,

정진하는 마음

부지런히

지혜의 혜가 밝아서

부동심을 이루도록

하옵소서.

Deluded thoughts of every kind,

when entrusted to our great unshakeable

mind,

will all melt away,

will all melt away.

Through mind, determination, and diligence

let me brighten and deepen my wisdom

and realize this great unshakeable mind.

눈이 눈이 우주에 가득 차 두루 밝아 밝아 또 밝아

모든 중생

한자리 한자리

한마음 한마음

한 몸 한 몸

만물이 함께 고苦에서 벗어나 벗어나

자유인이 되게 하옵소서.

세상을 바로 보게 하옵소서

큰 뜻을 이루게 하옵소서.

세상 계율 무위법을 벗어나지 않게 하옵소서

한 손 되게 하옵소서.

May the bright eye of wisdom fill the universe with light

shining brightly, illuminating all.

May all beings

become one, become one

one with all Buddhas

one mind, one mind

one body, one body.

May all beings

escape together

escape from suffering

and become free.

May I see the world as it truly is.

May I fulfill all of the great vows.

May I uphold the principles of the unseen realms as well as the rules of society.

May I become one hand.

나의 욕심을 떠나게 하옵소서

육신의 모든 습성을 녹이게 하는 능력이 생기게 하옵소서

큰 능력으로 나라를 돌보게 하옵소서

모습 없는 일체 영령들도 물질과 둘 아님을 알게 하옵소서

자성신의 뜻으로 모든 생활에서 항복받게 하옵소서.

일체제불이시여,

만 가지 꽃이 피고 만 가지 열매 익어 맛을 알게 하옵소서.

May I let go of my greed and desire.

May I develop the power to dissolve all habits of the body.

May I develop great spiritual ability and take care of the nation.

May I realize that all spirits of the dead,
though shapeless and unseen,
are not separate from this realm of form and matter.

May everything that arises in my life
surrender and follow
my inherent nature.

All Buddhas,
may ten thousand flowers bloom,
and ten thousand fruits ripen.
Let me know their true taste!

사방찬 四方讚

한마음을 찬탄하는 게송

한마음에

세상 도량

전부 들어 있으니

상대 경계 모두 놓아

이 마음이 구공이면

본래면목 계합되어

삼세가 다 구정토라

마음 비워 청정하면

세세생생

평안하리.

In Praise of One Mind

All places of inspiration and energy,

all places where enlightenment can be realized,

are found within one mind.

Just thoroughly entrust one mind

with everything that confronts me,

such that all discriminations and views

about myself and the world utterly disappear.

At that instant, I combine with my inherent nature

and the past, present, and future

are all the Buddha's Pure Land.

If my mind is thus empty and pure,

I will be at ease

in whatever place or time I find myself.

도량찬 道場讚

삼세심三世心이 일심一心으로
쉼 없이 돌아가는 도리를 찬탄함

일체 모든 부처님의 한마음은
더러웁고 깨끗함이 본래 없는 내 한마음일세.

삼세심三世心이 일심一心 되니
천지세상 그대로가
내 한마음 생활일세.

더럽다 깨끗하다
본래 없는 내 한마음 그대로가
여여한 법이로세.

부처님의 한마음은
유위법과 무위법을 한 손 안에 거머쥐고
만중생에게 대자비를 베푸시네.

**In praise of the truth
that my past, present, and future consciousness
always function together as one.**

The one mind of all Buddhas is my one mind,
inherently free of stained or pure.

My past consciousness
as an unenlightened being,
my present consciousness
as a being striving for enlightenment,
and my future consciousness
as an enlightened Buddha
will all become one,
and everything in the universe, just as it is,
will be the continuous flowing of my one mind.

Inherently free of all labels such as dirty or clean,
my one mind is utterly complete.
Just as it is,
it is the underlying truth
that supports everything in the universe.

Buddha's one mind holds all laws
of both the visible and the invisible realms,
and gives infinite compassion to all beings.

참회게 懺悔偈
참회하는 게송

제가 지은 모든 악업죄

선행 없는 모든 탐심죄

몸으로 입으로 뜻으로 지은 죄

일체 모든 잘못을

참회합니다.

Poem of Repentance

All harmful deeds I have committed,

all unwise actions

arising from greed and desire,

all harm

done through my body, speech, and thought,

I now repent of this

and all other harm I have caused.

참제업장십이존불 懺除業障十二尊佛
업장을 멸해 주시는 열두 분의 부처님

두루두루 겸손하온
마음 공덕 계율 법행 불

한마음의 보배로서
따뜻이 관하시어 살피시는 불

일체 모든 향기롭고 따뜻하온
마음의 불

광대무변
크신 뜻을 결정하온 불

Homage to the twelve Buddhas who dissolve all karma

The Buddha whose deep humility
gives rise to virtue, upright behavior,
and actions grounded in the Dharma.

The Buddha who uses the treasure of one mind
to gently observe and take care of all beings.

The Buddha endowed with every kind of fragrant
and gentle compassion.

The Buddha who makes decisions
of vast and inconceivable importance.

두루두루 위대하온 마음의 공덕 불

마음을 굳혀 세워 일체 모두 항복받아
태산 같은 업장들을 멸하신 불

넓고 밝은 한마음의 묘법음 법존 불

밝고 기쁜 마음의 손길 닿지 않는 곳 없는 불

The Buddha endowed with the virtue and merit
arising from a broad and harmonious mind.

The Buddha of great determination,
who subdues all obstacles,
and destroys mountains of karma.

The Buddha who venerates the Dharma,
transmitting the truth of bright and wide one mind.

The Buddha whose bright and joyful mind
touches every place.

무변하고 두루한 마음의 향 갖추신 불

사무 사유에 밝으신 불

밝고 밝은 마음 중심
걸림 없는 주 불

한마음의 보배는 두루 걸림 없이
굴림이 여여한 주 불

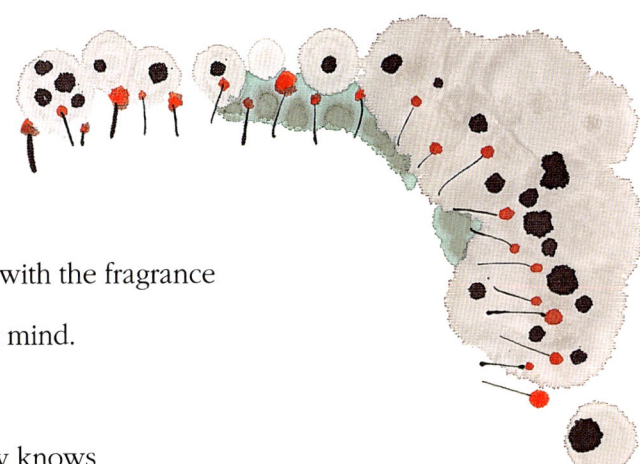

The Buddha who is infused with the fragrance

of limitless and omnipresent mind.

The Buddha who thoroughly knows

all states of existence and nonexistence.

The Supreme Buddha

who takes bright and bright mind as his center

and so is never entangled by anything.

The Supreme Buddha

one with everything

who applies the treasure of one mind to all things

without the least discrimination.

십악참회 十惡懺悔
열 가지 죄업을 참회함

살생한 큰 죄 오늘 참회합니다.

도둑질한 큰 죄 오늘 참회합니다.

사음한 큰 죄 오늘 참회합니다.

거짓말한 큰 죄 오늘 참회합니다.

삿된 말한 큰 죄 오늘 참회합니다.

이간질한 큰 죄 오늘 참회합니다.

나쁜 말한 큰 죄 오늘 참회합니다.

Repenting of the Ten Evil Actions

I now deeply repent of having killed.

I now deeply repent of having stolen.

I now deeply repent of sexually improper thoughts and behavior.

I now deeply repent of having lied.

I now deeply repent of having spoken manipulating words.

I now deeply repent of having spoken ill of others and caused discord among people.

I now deeply repent of having spoken harshly.

탐애한 큰 죄 오늘 참회합니다.
성낸 큰 죄 오늘 참회합니다.
어리석은 큰 죄 오늘 참회합니다.

백겁 천겁 쌓인 죄업
한생각에 사라지고
마른풀이 불에 타듯
남김없이 소멸되네.

I now deeply repent of having been overcome with desire and attachments.

I now deeply repent of having been angry.

I now deeply repent of having been ignorant and deluded.

With one thought,

evil karma accumulated

over endless eons disappears,

leaving nothing behind

like dry grass in a fire.

죄는 본래 자성 없고 마음 따라 일어나니

마음 만일 없어지면 죄업 또한 스러지네.

죄와 망심 모두 놓아 마음 모두 공하여야

이를 일러 이름하여 진실한 참회라하네.

Evil thoughts and actions do not just appear on their own.

They emerge according to the thoughts

I give rise to.

Thus, when those thoughts disappear

bad karma also vanishes.

While letting go of all wrong behaviors

and deluded thoughts,

if my mind becomes completely empty,

this can be called true repentance.

참회진언 懺悔眞言
죄업을 참회하는 진언

우리들의 삶의 길을 깨닫게 하여 주옵소서.

한마음의 크신 공덕 적정하게 항상 관하면
이 세상의 모든 재난 침범하지 못하리니
천상이나 인간이나 부처님의 복덕 받아
이 여의주 만난 이는 최상의 법 얻으리다.

천지의 만물 소생케 하는 도리천지
어머니이신 한마음에 귀의합니다.

The Mantra of Repentance

Let us awaken to how we should live, and become true human beings.

If I am always aware of and rely upon the great virtue and merit of one mind,
no disasters of this world can touch me, and I will receive the blessings of all Buddhas.
Whether a heavenly being or a human being,
anyone who meets this treasure, this one mind,
obtains the supreme Dharma.

I take refuge in one mind,
the mother of heaven and earth,
the giver of life to all things.

정법계진언 淨法界眞言
마음이 청정함을 관하는 진언

진정 올바른 행을 하리다.

호신진언 護身眞言
마음의 호법신은 일체 몸을 도우리다

진정 끊임없는 길

The mantra for realizing the inherent purity of mind

I will be upright and sincere in my behavior.

The Dharma protectors of mind take care of my body

Entrusting and letting go,
the truly limitless path.

관세음보살본심미묘육자대명왕진언
觀世音菩薩本心微妙六字大明王眞言

한마음의 미묘하온 마음의 작용을 보이신
여섯 자 진언

진정 내 마음으로

모든 악을

물리치게 하소서.

The mantra showing the profound and subtle functioning of one mind

Using mind,

may I completely dispel all evil.

준제진언 准提眞言

일체제불의 마음은 곧 내 한마음이므로
주인공 한마음을 관하는 진언

끝이 없는

마음의 계단 없는 계단을 넘어

진정코 마음의 구슬 굴리오리다.

제가 일체 한마음에 지성으로 관하오며

보리심을 내어서 크고 넓은 원을 세우오니

원컨대 저의 선정 지혜 속히 밝아지이다.

원컨대 저의 공덕 다 이루오리다.

원컨대 저의 복력 두루 장엄하여지이다.

원컨대 모든 중생 함께 성불하여지이다.

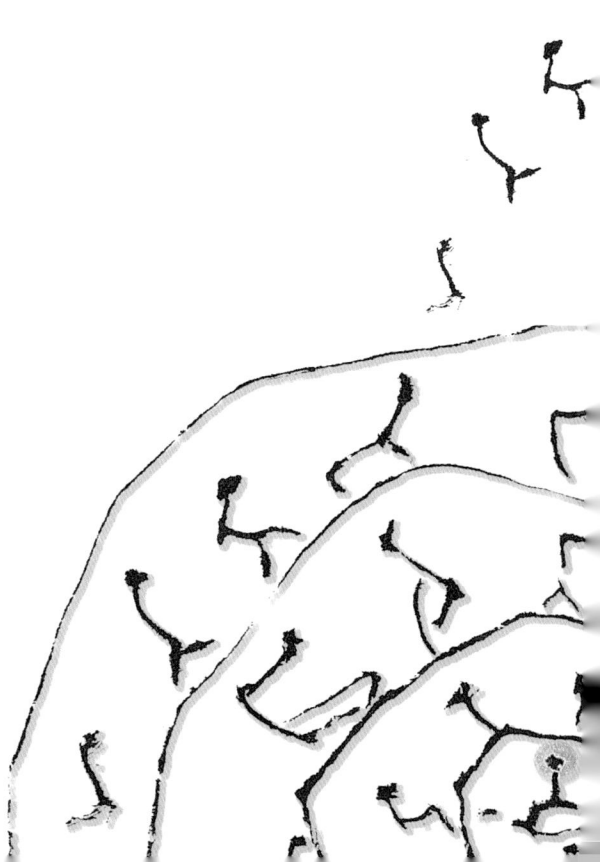

**The mantra for realizing one mind,
Juingong, which is itself the mind of all Buddhas.**

Mind,

with uncountable stages that are not fixed stages.

I will pass through these

and truly turn the great jewel of mind.

Sincerely entrusting everything to one mind,

determined to know the real and help all beings,

raising these great wishes,

may my samadhi wisdom swiftly brighten.

May I attain every kind of virtue.

May the blessings arising from my virtue

guide and sustain all beings.

May all beings together attain Buddhahood.

여래십대발원문 如來十大發願文
여래의 열 가지 큰 발원문

마음과 마음으로
삼악도를 여의옵기 원입니다.

마음의 탐 · 진 · 치를
어서 끊기 원입니다.

마음의 불 · 법 · 승을
항상 듣기 원입니다.

마음의 계 · 정 · 혜를
힘껏 닦기 원입니다.

The Ten Vows made by all Tathagatas

Using mind
through mind,
I vow to never again to be seduced
by the three evil states of consciousness.*

Greed, anger, and ignorance
existing within my mind,
I vow to dissolve without delay.

Buddha, Dharma, and Sangha
all live within my mind,
I vow to always listen to them.

Precepts, meditation, and wisdom
are all found within my mind,
I vow to ceaselessly cultivate them.

* These are the consciousness of hell beings, hungry ghosts, and animals.

둘 아닌 부처님 법 늘 배우기 원입니다.

마음에 보리심을 항상 내기 원입니다.

마음속의 극락세계 태어나기 원입니다.

마음속의 아미타불 속히 뵙기 원입니다.

온 세상에 나투기를 원입니다.

모든 중생 제도하길 원입니다.

The truth of non-duality,
taught by all Buddhas.
I vow to ceaselessly learn and practice.

I will know the real and attain enlightenment.
I vow to always sustain
and cultivate this determination.

Paradise is found within my mind,
I vow to attain it.

Amitabha Buddha
existing within my mind,
I vow to hurry and meet.

I vow to manifest throughout the entire world.

I vow to save all beings.

발사홍서원 發四弘誓願
네 가지 큰 원을 세움

가없는 중생을 다 건지오리다.

끝없는 번뇌를 다 녹이오리다.

한량없는 법문을 다 배우오리다.

위없는 불도를 다 이루오리다.

마음속의 모든 중생 맹세코 건지오리다.

마음속의 모든 번뇌 맹세코 녹이오리다.

마음속의 모든 법문 맹세코 배우오리다.

마음속의 모든 불도 맹세코 이루오리다.

Raising the Four Great Vows

Unenlightened beings beyond number, I will save.

Continuously arising delusions and defilements, I will dissolve.

The infinite teachings of the Dharma, I will learn.

Incomparable enlightenment, I will attain.

All unenlightened beings existing within me, I vow to save.

All delusions and defilements existing within me, I vow to dissolve.

All teachings of the Dharma, ever-present within me, I vow to learn.

Supreme enlightenment, inherent within me, I vow to attain.

발원이귀명례삼보
發願已歸命禮三寶

원을 발하여 한마음의 삼보님께 귀의합니다

시방에 항상 한마음으로 계신

부처님께 귀의합니다.

시방세계 항상 계신

진리에 귀의합니다.

시방세계 항상 계신

도량에 귀의합니다.

**Having given rise to these great vows,
I return to and rely upon
the Three Treasures of one mind.**

I take refuge in Buddha,
who is one with all,
in every place and
every dimension.

I take refuge in the truth,
ever-present throughout every realm.

I take refuge in the place for learning the truth.
Which is every place.

What follows is the traditional Korean version of *The Thousand Hands Sutra*.

천수경千手經 원문

다음의 천수경 표기 방식은 동국대학교 김호성 교수님의 자문을 참고로 하였습니다.

淨口業眞言

수리수리 마하수리 수수리 사바하 (세번)

五方內外安慰諸神眞言

나무 사만다 못다남 옴 도로도로 지미 사바하 (세번)

開經偈

無上甚深微妙法 百千萬劫難遭遇 我今聞見得受持 願解如來眞實意

開法藏眞言

옴 아라남 아라다 (세번)

千手千眼觀自在菩薩廣大圓滿無碍大悲心大陀羅尼啓請

稽首觀音大悲呪　願力弘深相好身　千臂莊嚴普護持　天眼光明遍觀照

眞實語中宣密語　無爲心內起悲心　速令滿足諸希求　永使滅除諸罪業

天龍衆聖同慈護　百千三昧頓薰修　受持身是光明幢　受持心是神通藏

洗滌塵勞願濟海　超證菩提方便門　我今稱誦誓歸依　所願從心悉圓滿

南無大悲觀世音　願我速知一切法　南無大悲觀世音　願我早得知慧眼

南無大悲觀世音　願我速度一切衆　南無大悲觀世音　願我早得善方便

南無大悲觀世音　願我速乘般若船　南無大悲觀世音　願我早得越苦海

南無大悲觀世音　願我速得戒定道　南無大悲觀世音　願我早登圓寂山

南無大悲觀世音 願我速會無爲舍 南無大悲觀世音 願我早同法性身

我若向刀山 刀山自摧折 我若向火湯 火湯自消滅 我若向地獄 地獄自枯渇

我若向餓鬼 餓鬼自飽滿 我若向修羅 惡心自調伏 我若向畜生 自得大智慧

南無觀世音菩薩摩訶薩 南無大勢至菩薩摩訶薩 南無千手菩薩摩訶薩

南無如意輪菩薩摩訶薩 南無大倫菩薩摩訶薩 南無觀自在菩薩摩訶薩

南無正趣菩薩摩訶薩 南無滿月菩薩摩訶薩 南無水月菩薩摩訶薩

南無軍茶利菩薩摩訶薩 南無十一面菩薩摩訶薩 南無諸大菩薩摩訶薩

南無本師阿彌陀佛(세번)

神妙章句大陀羅尼

나모라 다나다라 야야 나막알약 바로기제 새바라야 모지 사다바야

마하 사다바야 마하가로 니가야 옴 살바 바예수 다라나 가라야

다사명 나막 까리다바 이맘 알야 바로기제 새바라 다바 이라간타

나막 하리나야 마발다 이샤미 살발타 사다남 수반 아예염 살바

보다남 바바마라 미수다감 다냐타 옴 아로계 아로가 마지로가

지가란제 혜혜하례 마하 모지 사다바 사마라 사마라 하리나야

구로구로 갈마 사다야 사다야 도로도로 미연제 마하미연제 다라다라

다린나례 새바라 자라자라 마라미마라 아마라 몰제 예혜혜 로계

새바라 라아 미사미 나사야 나베 사미사미 나사야 모하자라 미사미

나사야 호로호로 마라호로 하레 바나마 나바 사라사라 시리시리

소로소로 못쟈못쟈 모다야 모다야 매다리야 니라간타 가마사 날사남

바라 하라나야 마낙 사바하 싯다야 사바하 마하 싯다야 사바하

싯다유예 새바라야 사바하 니라간타야 사바하 바라하 목카싱하

목카야 사바하 바나마 하따야 사바하 자가라 욕다야 사바하

상카섭나녜 모다나야 사바하 마하라 구타다라야 사바하 바마 사간타

이사 시체다 가릿나 이나야 사바하 먀가라 잘마 이바 사나야 사바하

나모라 다나다라 야야 나막알야 바로기제 새바라야 사바하 (세번)

四方讚

一灑東方潔道場　二灑南方得淸凉　三灑西方俱淨土　四灑北方永安康

道場讚

道場淸淨無瑕穢　三寶天龍降此地　我今持誦妙眞言　願賜慈悲密加護

懺悔偈

我昔所造諸惡業　皆由無始貪瞋痴　從身口意之所生　一切我今皆懺悔

懺除業障十二尊佛

南無懺除業障寶勝藏佛　寶光王火炎照佛　一切香火自在力王佛　百億恒河沙決定佛

振威德佛　金剛堅强消伏壞散佛　普光月殿妙音尊王佛　歡喜藏摩尼寶積佛

無盡香勝王佛　獅子月拂　歡喜莊嚴珠王佛　帝寶幢摩尼勝光佛

十惡懺悔

殺生重罪今日懺悔　偸盜重罪今日懺悔　邪淫重罪今日懺悔　妄語重罪今日懺悔

綺語重罪今日懺悔　兩舌重罪今日懺悔　惡口重罪今日懺悔　貪愛重罪今日懺悔

瞋恚重罪今日懺悔　痴暗重罪今日懺悔　百劫積集罪　一念頓蕩盡　如火焚枯草

滅盡無有餘　罪無自性從心起　心若滅時罪亦亡　罪亡心滅兩俱空　是則名爲眞懺悔

懺悔眞言

옴 살바 못자 모지 사다야 사바하 (세번)

准提功德聚　寂情心常訟　一切諸大難　無能侵是人
天上及人間　壽福如佛等　遇此如意珠　定獲無等等
南無七俱胝佛母大准提菩薩 (세번)

淨法界眞言
옴 남 (세번)

護身眞言
옴 치림 (세번)

觀世音菩薩本心微妙六字大明王眞言
옴 마니 반메 훔 (세번)

准提眞言
나모 사다남 삼막 삼못다 구치남 다냐타
〈옴 자례 주례 준제 사바하 부림〉 (세번)

我今持誦大准提　即發菩提廣大願　願我定慧速圓明
願我功德皆成就　願我勝福遍莊嚴　願共衆生成佛道

如來十大發願文

願我永離三惡道　願我速斷貪瞋痴　願我常聞佛法僧　願我勤修戒定慧

願我恒隨諸佛學　願我不退菩提心　願我決定生安養　願我速見阿彌陀

願我分身遍塵刹　願我廣度諸衆生

發四弘誓願

衆生無邊誓願度　煩惱無盡誓願斷　法門無量誓願學　佛道無上誓願成

自性衆生誓願度　自性煩惱誓願斷　自性法門誓願學　自性佛道誓願成

發願已 歸命禮三寶

南無常住十方佛　南無常住十方法　南無常住十方僧　(세번)

About the Artist

It was said of old that as one becomes closer to the Dao, the path of truth, one becomes more pure and open, and this can be clearly seen in the works of Hyo Rim. Approaching art as meditation, he strives to express basic aspects of our true nature - openness, love, tolerance, wisdom, and our connection with all existence. Yet as he explores these, we can still feel his love of ordinary people and his hopes for them. He conveys all of this to paint and paper, where it waits with a quiet power, ready to remind the viewer of the warmth and wisdom inherent within us all.

One of Korea's foremost modern artists, Hyo Rim has won numerous awards and participated in over 200 exhibitions around the world. A professional artist for the past 30 years, he also teaches art at Hongik University, which is widely considered Korea's preeminent school of Fine Arts and Design.

임효 작가(作家)에 대하여

작가 임효는 1955년 전북 정읍출생으로 홍익대학교 미술대학과 동 교육대학원을 졸업했다.
2004년까지 모두 14회에 이르는 개인전을 가졌고, 85년 국립현대미술관의 "청년작가초대전,"
98년 "서울 미술대전 주거 공간의 미", 독일과 헝가리에서 열린 "동방의 빛 I "전과 러시아에서 열린 "동방의 빛 II "전 등
국내외에서 활발하게 전시를 개최해왔다. 또한 2005년 7월에는 세종문화회관 전관에서 화업 30년 전을 개최하기도 하였다.
수상경력으로 동아미술상, 선미술상 수상이 있으며 호는 호산(湖山)이다.

도(道)에 가까워 질수록 단순해진다는 옛 선사의 말씀대로라면 임효 작가는 그 경지에 다가가고 있다고 할 수 있다.
갈수록 단출해지는 점과 선과 면만을 사용하여 그는 관용과 용서, 넉넉함과 여유로움, 세간을 따뜻하게 품으면서도 출세간의
도리를 향한 부단한 모색과 같은, 우리의 영혼 속에 뿌리 깊게 내면화된 동양정신의 진수를 함축적으로 화폭에 담아 낸다.
그러나 축약된 간결함 속에서도 인간 삶의 깊이와 폭을 우리가 항상 돌아가 안기고 싶은 고향의 품처럼 푸근한 마음으로
정감있게 그려낸다. 그래서, 그의 그림은 따스하다. 관세음보살의 대자비심이 고스란히 화폭에 옮겨진 듯 천수경에 실린
그의 작품 속에서 우리는 편안함과 따뜻한 보살핌을 한껏 느낄 수 있다.

Artist's Postscript
Hyo Rim

When I was first approached about doing the illustrations for Seon Master Daehaeng's *A Thousand Hands of Compassion,* I couldn't imagine how it could be done. It was that overwhelming. The depths of meaning in *A Thousand Hands of Compassion* are so profound that I couldn't imagine how my brushes could express them.

I started listening to recordings of *A Thousand Hands of Compassion* in my car and in my studio. At the same time, I also read every book I could find about the traditional interpretations of this sutra. Unfortunately, the more I listened and read, the more stressed I felt! I began to worry that I wouldn't be able to create a single image, or that I would end up painting something out of haste and desperation.

It was then that the meanings of what I had been listening to began to seep down within me. It was then that I realized that my paintings weren't done by "me." They're done by some thing deeper; "The Buddha's grace" is as good a name as any. I could hear Seon Master Daehaeng telling me, "Entrust everything you do to inherent one mind." As I did this, the paintings began to flow, done by something far beyond this sense of "I."

작가(作家) 후기
임효

대행큰스님의 『뜻으로 푼 천수경』 영한본(英韓本)에 들어갈 그림을 그려달라는 부탁을 맨 처음 받았을 때,
제가 느꼈던 마음의 무게란 정말이지 말로 형언하기 어려웠습니다. 앞으로 천리 만리 길을 가야만 한다는 아득함이
몰려왔습니다. 천수경의 이치가 높고 깊어 그 속에 담긴 뜻을 화필로 옮기기엔 너무나 먼 세계라고 느껴졌기 때문입니다.

우선 천수경과 친해지기 위해 자동차에서도 작업실에서도 『뜻으로 푼 천수경』 테이프를 틀어놓고 듣기를
반복하였습니다. 또 천수경의 뜻을 보다 더 많이 이해하기 위해서 천수경에 관한 책이라면 손에 닿는 대로 구입하여
탐독하였습니다. 그러나, 그렇게 하면 할 수록 그림 그리는 일에 대한 부담이 커지더니, 급기야는 스트레스가 극에 달해
가슴을 내리누르는 압박감이 덮쳐왔습니다. 이러다가는 한 장의 그림도 못 그리겠다는 생각이 들면서 성급하게
그림을 그려보겠다는 의지를 보인 것이 후회 막심한 적도 많았습니다.

그러던 중, 서서히 제 안에서 이런 생각이 들기 시작했습니다. '이것은 내가 하는 일이 아니라 부처님의 원력으로 하는
일이다.' 이러한 믿음이 제 마음과 몸 속 구석구석에 퍼져나가면서, 대행큰스님의 가르침이 제 귀에 울려 퍼졌습니다.
"일체의 모든 일을 다 한마음에 놓아라." 제가 스님 말씀처럼 한마음에 맡겨 놓고 그리기 시작하자,
그림은 물 흘러가듯 그려지기 시작했고, '나' 아닌 내가 그림을 완성할 수 있었습니다.

2008년 9월 임효 합장

Anyang Headquarters of Hanmaum Seonwon

101-62, Seoksu-dong, Anyang-si Gyeonggi-do,
430-040, Republic of Korea
Tel : 82-31-470-3175 / Fax : 82-31-471-6928
http://www.hanmaum.org/eng
Email : onemind@hanmaum.org

Overseas Branches of Hanmaum Seonwon

ARGENTINA
Buenos Aires
Miró 1575, cp(1406) Cap. Fed. Rep. Argentina
Tel : 54-11-4921-9286 / Fax : 54-11-4921-9286
http://www.hanmaumtuc.org
Email : hanmaumbsas@hotmail.com

Tucumán
Av. Aconquija 5250, El Corte, Yerba Buena,
cp(4107) Tucumán, Rep. Argentina
Tel : 54-381-425-1400
http://www.hanmaumtuc.org
Email : hanmaumtuc@arnet.com.ar

BRASIL
Sao Paulo
R. Newton Prado 540, Bom Retiro
Sao Paulo, C.P. 01127-000, Brasil
Tel: (55-11)3337-5291

CANADA
Toronto
20 Mobile Dr. North York, Ontario M4H 1H9, Canada
Tel : 1-416-750-7943 / Fax : 1-416-701-1359
http://www.hanmaumcanada.org/eng.htm
Email : hanmaum@hanmaumcanada.org

GERMANY
Kaarst
Broicherdorf Str. 102, 41564 Kaarst, Germany
Tel : 49-2131-969551 / Fax : 49-2131-969552
http://www.hanmaum-zen.de
Email : hanmaum@t-online.de

THAILAND
Bangkok
86-1 soi 4 Sukhumvit 63, Bangkok, Thailand
Tel : 66-2-391-0091
http://home.hanmaum.org/bangkok
Email : hanmaumbkk@hanmail.net

USA
Chicago
7852 N. Lincoln Ave., Skokie, IL 60077, USA
Tel : 1-847-674-0811 / Fax : 1-847-674-0811
http://www.buddhapia.com/hmu/chi/
Email : hanmaumchicago@yahoo.com

Los Angeles
1905 S. Victoria Ave., L.A., CA 90016, USA
Tel : 1-323-766-1316 / Fax : 1-323-766-1916
Email : lahanmaum@hanmaum.org

New York
144-39, 32 Ave., Flushing, NY 11354, USA
Tel : 1-718-460-2019 / Fax : 1-718-939-3974
Email : nyhanmaum@yahoo.com

Washington D. C.
7807 Trammel Rd. Annandale, VA 22003, USA
Tel : 1-703-560-5166 / Fax : 1-703-560-5566
http://home.hanmaum.org/
Email : juingong_dc@yahoo.com

한마음선원 본원   (우)430-040 경기도 안양시 만안구 석수동 101-62
Tel : 82-31-470-3100   Fax : 82-31-470-3116
Website : http://www.hanmaum.org
Email : onemind@hanmaum.org

국내지원

광명선원   (우)369-900 충청북도 음성군 금왕읍 무극4구 산5-2
TEL:(043)877-5000   FAX:(043)877-2900

제주지원   (우)690-140 제주도 제주시 영평동 1500
TEL:(064)727-3100   FAX:(064)727-0302

부산지원   (우)606-080 부산광역시 영도구 동삼동 522-1
TEL:(051)403-7077   FAX:(051)403-1077

광주지원   (우)502-270 광주광역시 서구 치평동 201-5
TEL:(062)373-8801   FAX:(062)373-0174

울산지원   (우)683-500 울산광역시 북구 천곡동 927-7
TEL:(052)295-2335   FAX:(052)295-2336

대구지원   (우)706-838 대구광역시 수성구 중동 532-274
TEL:(053)767-3100   FAX:(053)765-1600

중부경남   (우)621-802 경상남도 김해시 진영읍 방동리 321-1
TEL:(055)345-9900   FAX:(055)346-2179

진주지원   (우)660-941 경상남도 진주시 미천면 오방리 50
TEL:(055)746-8163   FAX:(055)746-7825

공주지원   (우)314-870 충청남도 공주시 사곡면 신영3리 152-3
TEL:(041)852-9100   FAX:(041)852-9105

포항지원   (우)791-220 경상북도 포항시 북구 우현동 13-1
TEL:(054)232-3163   FAX:(054)241-3503

청주지원   (우)360-814 충청북도 청주시 상당구 우암동 295-7
TEL:(043)259-5599   FAX:(043)255-5599

강릉지원   (우)210-940 강원도 강릉시 포남2동 1304
TEL:(033)651-3003   FAX:(033)652-0281

통영지원   (우)650-110 경상남도 통영시 도천동 113-3
TEL:(055)643-0643   FAX:(055)643-0642

목포지원   (우)530-490 전라남도 목포시 상동 952-19
TEL:(061)284-1771   FAX:(061)284-1770

문경지원   (우)745-823 경상북도 문경시 산양면 반곡리 449번지
TEL:(054)555-8871   FAX:(054)556-1989

Books by Hanmaum Publications

- A Thousand Hands of Compassion <Bilingual, Korean/English>
  만가지 꽃이 피고 만가지 열매 익어
- Wake Up and Laugh! <English>
- No River to Cross, No Raft to Find <English>
- It's Hard to Say <English>
- My Heart is a Golden Buddha <English>
- Practice in Daily Life : Series <Bilingual, Korean/English>
  생활속의 참선수행 시리즈
  1) To Discover True Self, "I" Must Die 죽어야 나를 보리라
  2) Walking Without a Trace 함이 없이 하는 도리
  3) Let Go and Observe 맡겨 놓고 지켜봐라
  4) Mind, Treasure House of Happiness
     마음은 보이지 않는 행복의 창고
  5) The Furnace Within Yourself 일체를 용광로에 넣어라
- 건널 강이 어디 있으랴 <Korean>
- 내 마음은 금부처 <Korean>
- El Camino Interior <Spanish>
- Vida de la Maestra Seon Daehaeng <Spanish>
- Enseñanzas de la Maestra Daehaeng <Spanish>
- Wo immer du bist, ist Buddha <German>
- 人生不是苦海 <Simplified Chinese>

Books available through other publishers

- No River to Cross 건널 강이 어디 있으랴 〈영문판〉
  — Wisdom Publications, U.S.A

- Wie fließendes Wasser 내 마음은 금부처 〈독일어판〉
  — Goldmann Arkana, Germany

- Ningún Río Que Cruzar
  건널 강이 어디 있으랴 〈스페인어판〉
  — Kailas Editorial S.L., Spain

- Umarmt von Mitgefühl
  만가지 꽃이 피고 만가지 열매 익어 〈독일어판〉
  — Diederichs-Random House, Germany
  (2009. 9월 출시예정)

- Vertraue und Lass Alles Los
  건널 강이 어디 있으랴 〈독일어판〉
  — Goldman Arkana-Random House, Germany
  (2010. 4월 출시예정)

- 내 마음은 금부처 〈번자체 대만판〉
  橡樹林文化出版
  — Taiwan (2009. 10월 출시예정)

한마음국제문화원
한 마 음 출 판 사

Hanmaum International Culture Institute
Hanmaum Publications

*If you would like more information about these
books or would like to order copies of them,
please call or write to:*

101-60, Seoksu-dong, Manan-gu, Anyang-si,
Gyeonggi-do, 430-040, Republic of Korea
Tel : (82-31) 470-3175
Fax: (82-31) 471-6928
e-mail : onemind@hanmaum.org

경기도 안양시 만안구 석수동 101-60
전화 : 031-470-3175
팩스 : 031-470-6928

책에 관한 문의나 주문은 위의 연락처로 연락주시기 바랍니다.